*Little Book of*

# HEIRLOOM CHRISTMAS TREE DECORATIONS

*Little Book of*

# HEIRLOOM CHRISTMAS TREE DECORATIONS

## JENNY STEPHENSON

SALLYMILNER
PUBLISHING

First published in 2003 by
Sally Milner Publishing Pty Ltd
PO Box 2104
Bowral NSW 2576
AUSTRALIA

© Jenny Stephenson 2003

Design and stitch illustrations: Anna Warren, Warren Ventures Pty Ltd
Editing: Anne Savage
Photography: Tim Connolly

Printed in China

National Library of Australia Cataloguing-in-Publication data:

Stephenson, Jenny.
    Little book of heirloom Christmas tree decorations.

    ISBN 1 86351 312 4.

    1. Christmas decorations.  2. Embroidery.  I. Title.
    (Series : Milner craft series).


    745.59412

10  9  8  7  6  5  4  3  2  1

# Contents

# Introduction

This little tree came into being as a result of a friend admiring a similar one I had made for my family many years ago. Her pleas to 'teach me how to make it' led to the development of the current design, to classes at the sister shops The Calico House and Ivy and Maude in Perth, and ultimately to this little book.

The layout of the book follows the sequence I follow in classes. It involves an element of delayed gratification—one has to wait a while to see many of the decorations finished. This is done not to create frustration but to reduce it! It is amazing how often your thread will catch on beads or sequins sewn on too soon, 'just to see how it will look'!

Although the instructions may appear extremely precise, there is much scope for doing your own thing. Different fabrics can be used for the balls and bells, beads can be chosen to suit your own prefer-

ences, or perhaps you have some tiny trinkets that have been secreted away for that special project.

An heirloom is something which has been handed down from generation to generation. Perhaps it is a little presumptuous to call this project an heirloom for, strictly, it has not yet qualified. As this tree grew, I based many of the decorations on those we hang on our large Christmas tree each year. The little glass birds, the gingerbread man made by one of my sons at kindergarten, the snowman sticker left on the children's bedroom door the year we had Christmas with friends in Scotland—these and other treasures are represented here. Including such reminders of Christmases past contributes towards your tree becoming a true family tree and, for the future, a family heirloom.

I hope you enjoy stitching it.

JENNY

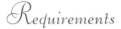

# Requirements

Although specific materials have been listed, these can of course be altered to suit your own preferences.

## FABRICS

50 x 25 cm (20 x 10 inches) dark green silk satin or similar

silk satin or silk-like lining fabrics as follows:
  10 x 12.5 cm (4 x 5 inches) red
  10 cm (4 inch) squares of royal blue, golden green, bottle green, yellow, and white
  5 cm (2 inch) squares of turquoise and burgundy

16 cm (6 ½ inch) square of gold paper silk, lining fabric or organza for the stumpwork star (this must be a fabric that appears the same on each side)

## THREADS AND RIBBONS

DMC Art. 282 (Light Gold), Art. 283 (Light Silver) and Art. 270 (Red) or similar 3-ply metallic embroidery threads. Two strands of stranded metallic thread could be used in place of these threads, e.g. DMC 5282 (Gold), 5283 (Silver) and 5270 (Red)

DMC stranded metallic thread 5269 (Green)

DMC stranded cotton 436 (Teddy Brown) and 729 (Honey Gold)

DMC Rayon R581 (Grasshopper Green)

Kreinik 2 mm (1⁄16 inch) ribbon in 001 (Silver), 002 (Gold), 102 (Vatican Gold) and 003 (Red)

Kreinik fine braid No.8 033 (Royal Blue)

Kreinik blending filaments 003 (Red), 032 (Pearl), 027 (Orange) and 019 (Pewter)

Machine metallic embroidery thread No.40 in Silver, Gold, Red and Royal Blue

Madeira monofilament no. 60 (Col. 1001) or similar invisible thread

Rajmahal Art silks, colours 29 (Charcoal), 96 (White), 44 (Tangier Sand), 45 (Baby Camel), 113 (Purple Dusk), 126 (Royal Blue), 152 (Spring Leaf), 175 (Earth), 181 (Gentle Magenta), 255 (Vermilion), 788 (Perfect Blue). (See page 95 for DMC equivalents if Rajmahal silks not readily available.)

Ribbon floss, golden yellow (to cover tub)

Hand/machine-sewing thread to match dark green of foundation silk

Hand/machine-sewing thread to contrast with dark green of foundation silk

## BEADS

Size 11 glass seed beads: Mill Hill 2011 (Victorian Gold), 20557 (Old Gold), 2013 (Red), 20332 (Emerald), 20167 (Christmas Green), 20161 (Crystal), 0020 (Royal Blue), 02006 (Ice Blue), 2062 (Crayon Red), 2058 (Crayon White)

Mill Hill antique glass seed beads 03049 (Rich Red)

Size 15 glass seed beads: Mill Hill petite glass beads 40557 (Old Gold), 40479 (White)

Delica beads: Maria George DBR43 (Silver-lined Red), Maria George DBR35 (Silver)

11 mm (⅜ inch) bugle beads, twisted: Maria George TW/B 20 (Silver)

6 mm (¼ inch) bugle beads: Mill Hill small bugle beads 72011 (Victorian Gold), 72052 (Red Velvet); Maria George #3, col. 16 (Lime) and col. 18 (Yellow Gold)

3 mm best quality gold pearl beads

3 mm best quality silver pearl beads

2 mm best quality gold pearl beads

Two 4 mm white pearl beads

3 mm white pearl beads

One 6 mm (¼ inch) topaz Austrian cut-crystal bead

Flat-backed sew-on crystals

Mill Hill Crystal Treasures (animals and snowflakes)

## SEQUINS (SPANGLES)

3 or 4 mm in gold, silver, green and red. (Tiny sequins of good quality are becoming increasingly difficult to obtain. Only a small number are used in this project and you may find what you need in a mixed packet. Sequins can be replaced with a cluster of seed beads, one bead larger than suggested for the particular star or ball, or tiny star sequins.)

5 and 6 mm cup sequins in gold, silver, green and red

6 mm flat sequins, gold

8 mm flat sequins, red

10 mm flat sequins, gold and silver

Small quantity of assorted coloured sequins for fill-ins

## OTHER MATERIALS

Miniature tub, approx. 4 cm (1½ inches) high. (Suitable objects include large wooden beads, miniature terracotta flowerpots, and wooden candleholders.)

20 cm (8 inches) of 34 gauge beading wire

30 gauge paper-covered cake decorating wire (for stumpwork star)

110 gsm photocopy paper or cartridge paper

20 x 30 cm (8 x 12 inch) piece of medium-weight iron-on VileneTM (interfacing)

13 cm (5 in) square of template
plastic or firm cardboard

Tissue paper

Fibre-fill (soft toy stuffing)

## EQUIPMENT

In addition to your usual
embroidery tools you will need
the following:

Size 7, 10 and 12 crewel needles

Size 10 and 12 sharps needles

Silk or wedding-dress pins

10 cm (4 inch) embroidery hoop

Light-coloured pencil or air-
soluble fine-point marking pen

Black fine-point fibre pen

Scissors suitable for cutting paper,
metallic threads and fine wire

Fine-nosed pliers

Eyebrow tweezers

# Order of working

The embroidery and beading of the tree is carried out in layers following the preparation of the foundation shape.

The first layer—the garland, stars and snowflakes—consists of embroidery using metallic threads which, as well as creating reference points for the placement of other motifs, helps to stabilise the fabric on to the foundation paper.

The second layer comprises the embroidery of tiny novelty decorations such as angels and birds directly on to the silk foundation.

In the third layer the balls and bells are made separately, then appliquéd onto the foundation.

The final layer involves most of the beading and the filling in of unwanted spaces with tiny stars, snowflakes, beads and sequins.

Lastly, a three-dimensional stumpwork treetop star is made and inserted during the final assembly of your miniature heirloom tree.

## GENERAL INSTRUCTIONS FOR EMBROIDERY

### KEY TO EMBROIDERY THREADS

To save endless repetition of their full names, threads throughout are indicated by a letter or letters and a number as follows:

DG  DMC light gold/fil or clair or any similar 3-ply metallic thread

DS  DMC light silver/fil argent clair or any similar 3-ply metallic thread

DR  DMC red/rouge or any similar 3-ply metallic thread

S  Metallic No.40 sewing thread, Silver

G     Metallic No.40 sewing thread, Gold

R     Metallic No.40 sewing thread, Red

B     Metallic No.40 sewing thread, Blue

K     Kreinik blending filament, e.g. K019 = Kreinik blending filament, pewter

KB     Kreinik fine braid

KR     Kreinik 2 mm (1/16 inch) ribbon

RJ     Rajmahal Art Silk, e.g. RJ96 = Rajmahal 96 (White)

D     DMC stranded threads, e.g. D436 = DMC 436, Teddy Brown

D581r     DMC Rayon, Grasshopper Green

D5269     DMC stranded metallic, Green

## USING METALLIC THREADS

Metallic threads are used extensively in the embroidery of this tree. I find the following guidelines useful in achieving the best results.

Like other threads, metallic threads do seem to have a grain; they feel smoother when run between the fingers from one end than from the other. Thread the end from which the feeling is smoother through the needle. When working with reeled thread such as the DMC 3-ply thread, thread the end that comes from the reel.

The actual process of passing the thread through the fabric does cause wear on the thread. This can result in an annoying habit of catching and stripping. The following strategies help to reduce this:

• Use a needle that is large enough to make a hole in the fabric that the thread will pass through easily without catching. A no.7 crewel or embroidery needle is the smallest I would use for 3-ply metallic threads.

- Use short lengths of thread— about 30–35 cm (12–14 inches) of working thread once threaded in the needle.

- Keep the tail short—the needle will wear through the thread at the point at which it sits in the eye. Letting it out as you run short of working thread allows this worn area to pass through the fabric and results in catching. Start with the length of tail with which you are happy to finish.

- If the thread catches, unthread the needle and run the thread through your fingers from the fabric to the thread end. Repeating this several times will fix the problem if you do it the first time it catches. If the problem persists, finish off at the back of your work and replace the thread. (Don't throw these odd lengths away—you can use a single ply of the thread for filling in spaces with tiny stars later.)

- Stab stitching will help the threads to pass through all layers of the foundation more easily than will a scooping stitch. Stitching through all layers also helps stabilise the silk background on the foundation paper.

- Use a knot! Once assembled, you will not be able to get to the back of your work again. Knots will not show through and will ensure your threads are secured.

Use a smaller needle, crewel size 10 or 12, for machine metallic thread.

# GENERAL INSTRUCTIONS FOR BEADING

## USING INVISIBLE THREAD

All beading in this project is done with invisible thread (monofilament). I prefer to use this as it allows the light to catch the full colour and sparkle of the beads. An added advantage is that you don't have to keep changing your thread to match the colour of the beads. Use a size 10 or 12 sharps needle.

Always work with a double thread. If used singly, the thread seems to fall out of the needle eye and, if pulled firmly, will bounce back into ringlets! Using a doubled length knotted at the end reduces the curling and the thread will stay threaded. I also re-knot the end of the thread as soon as I have cut it off after beading. This saves rethreading and it is easier to find when next you need it.

## BEADING

Although instructions for beading each little ornament are given throughout the book, it is advisable to leave beading of the stars and snowflakes until after the baubles and bells have been appliquéd onto the foundation. This eliminates the risk of your threads catching on the beads during the rest of the surface embroidery.

It is important to secure the thread firmly after stitching the first bead or bead and sequin combination. For example, to stitch a bead and sequin combination, thread the needle with a doubled length of invisible thread, bringing the needle up

*Figure 1*

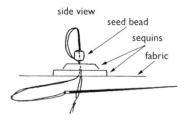

side view

seed bead

sequins

fabric

where the beading is required. Do not pull it through completely, leaving about a centimetre of thread at the back (figure 1). Thread the sequin on to the needle followed by the seed bead. Now, take the thread back through the sequin to the back of the work and thread it through the gap in the double thread between the knot and the foundation.

Pull the thread through firmly, checking that the bead and sequin are now sitting flush with the silk. Secure the thread by taking a small backstitch in the Vilene TM before moving on to attach the next bead.

This technique of anchoring the thread is recommended whenever a new thread is used in the beading.

Further beads are sewn on simply by bringing the needle up at the point where you want the bead to be, threading on the bead and inserting the needle down to the back of the work. It is not necessary to secure after each following bead is attached.

I am often asked how to make seed beads sit in a particular way. If you want the bead to sit on its side, attach it with a stitch approximately the length of the bead. If the needle is returned to the back through the same hole that it came up, the bead will tend to sit with the hole uppermost.

Bugle beads look like tiny cylinders. Bring the needle up where one end of the bead is to be placed, thread the bead on to the needle and let it slip down the thread to the fabric. Hold it in place with your thumb and take the thread down at the other end of the bead.

*Tip* Spreading your beads out on a piece of fabric such as felt or velvet helps to keep them under control when beading. Pick the bead up with your needle. This is easier than picking up with your fingers before threading. It also helps protect the finish on some metallic beads that can be affected by skin oils.

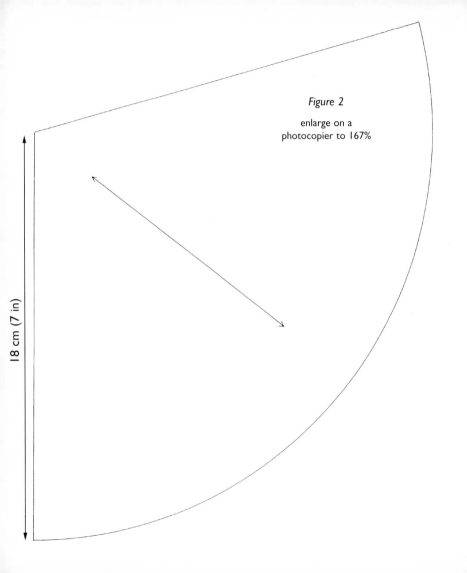

*Figure 2*

enlarge on a
photocopier to 167%

18 cm (7 in)

# Preparing the foundation shape

1. Photocopy foundation shape (figure 2) at 167%. Iron VileneTM to the back of the paper (the side with the markings) ensuring that it has adhered firmly. This makes the foundation firmer as well as giving a better surface for anchoring threads. Cut around shape carefully, keeping the edges smooth.

2. Lay the silk out flat, wrong side up. Using the cut-out shape as a template, lay this on the fabric, noting the direction of the grain, and trace around it with a light-coloured pencil. Leaving a seam allowance of about 12 mm (½ inch) all round, cut out the shape from the fabric. Although this can be done satisfactorily with ordinary scissors, I prefer to use pinking shears in order to minimise fraying.

3. Pin the cut-out shape to the wrong side of the silk, ensuring foundation shape is placed centrally and seam allowances are equal on all sides (figure 3a).

4. Starting at the bottom of one edge and working towards the apex, turn the seam allowance over along the straight edge and tack in place through all layers. Make sure you form a neat fold at the apex of the shape before tacking down the second side. A neat fold is important in order to get a tidy seam when you finally assemble your tree. Secure and cut thread (figure 3b).

5. Starting with a knot on the right side of the fabric, run a row of small gathering stitches around the curved edge of the fabric close to the edge, and across the folded-in side edges, as shown in figure 3b. Fold up

and pin both ends to the sides as shown in figure 3c—this prevents the ends curling up in the next step.

6. Pull up the gathering thread—this will draw the fabric up over the curved edge of the paper shape and cover it. Fasten off gathering thread. Adjust gathers.

7. Stitch turned curved edge to turned side-seam allowances at each end of the curved edge.

8. Hold turned-up allowance in place with small tacking stitches, taking the thread through all layers around and close to the curved edge (figure 3d).

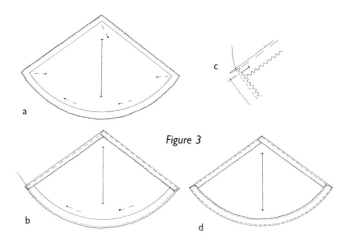

Figure 3

This forms the foundation of your tree. Check that the shape is flat and is covered smoothly, the edges are firm and the corner turns are as flat and neat as you can get them. Most of the embroidery is done on this foundation and working on something so stiff will feel a little awkward at first.

It is important that the shape be kept as free of wrinkles as possible, so try to hold it flat while sewing rather than bunching it up.

# Layer 1: Garland, stars and snowflakes

1. Photocopy figure 4 at 167%. Trace the outline of the foundation shape and the garland lines onto tissue paper. This is best done with a fine fibre-point pen.

2. Matching all three edges, pin in place on the right side of the silk-covered foundation.

3. Starting at one edge, outline the position of one of the scalloped garland lines by stitching through both the tissue paper and the silk with small running stitches in a contrasting colour. Finish thread off firmly at end. Outline the second garland line in the same manner.

4. Gently tear away tissue paper to reveal stitching lines on the silk.

Scoring the paper along the stitch line with the needle will make this easier.

### GARLAND

This is done in alternating chain stitch. Thread a size 7 crewel needle with equal lengths of both DG and DR, knotting both threads together at end. Starting at one side edge, and using a stab stitching approach, stitch through all layers.

As you approach the end of each row of stitching, curl the side edges of the foundation around to ensure the ends of the stitched garlands will match up on the seam line. Adjust the last few stitches if necessary.

*Tip* Run a soft white or yellow pencil over the line of running stitches. This will mark the spaces between the stitches and give you another guideline to follow when the stitches are removed during the embroidery.

## STARS AND
## SNOWFLAKES

Mark positions of stars and snowflakes.

1. Using tissue paper as before, trace the outline of the foundation shape, the garland lines and all the stars and snowflakes from figure 4. Ignore all other markings.

2. Pin the tracing to the foundation, matching side edges and garland lines.

3. Using tiny straight stitches in a contrasting colour, as before, mark in the position of the points of each star. Start each stitch at the end of the point and insert again 1–2 mm (no more than ⅟₁₆ inch) away from the point, outside the area to be embroidered (figure 5). You will stitch each star inside these marks. Complete marking each star or snowflake before moving on to the next.

4. Gently tear away paper.

Each star and snowflake has been numbered (see figure 4). Following general directions for each particular shape, specific instructions for the embroidery and beading of each are given. For ease of stitching the following two layers, the novelty decorations and

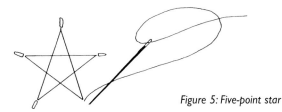

*Figure 5: Five-point star*

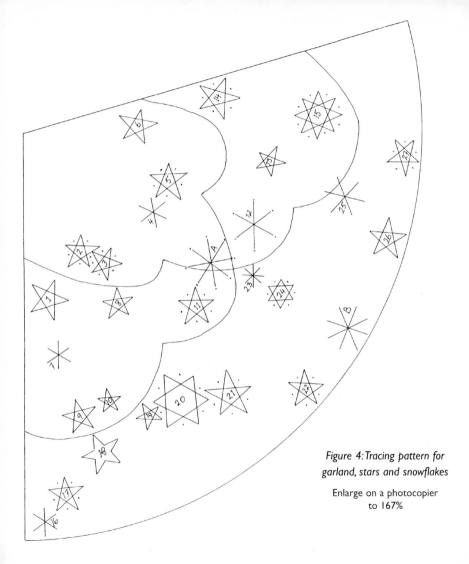

*Figure 4: Tracing pattern for garland, stars and snowflakes*

Enlarge on a photocopier to 167%

the balls and bells, all beading should be left until the balls and bells of layer 3 have been appliquéd.

Most of the stars are based on a simple five-point shape, but some six-point and eight-point stars are also included. The drawn outlines on figure 4 indicate the form each star will take.

Stars are worked in a stab-stitch manner through all layers. Once the main outline of the star has been stitched, the tacking markers can be removed.

For clarity, the instructions are illustrated with symmetrically shaped stars. Note that many stars in the actual design are drawn as being, and are meant to be, asymmetrical (figure 6d)

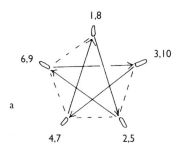

*Figure 6*

d  asymmetrical star

## BASIC FIVE-POINT STAR

This star is worked in straight stitches sewn in the order shown in figure 6a.

Bring needle up at 1 and down at 2. Keeping the stitch firm, move back one space, bringing the needle up again at 3. Take the next stitch across the previous one and insert the needle at 4.

Continue in this fashion until needle is brought up at 9 ready to make the last stitch.

Before inserting at 10, pass the needle under the thread running from 1 to 2. This will result in the star having a woven appearance with no loose long threads. The stitching of the finished star should be interwoven as shown in figure 6b.

If a second round is to be stitched, bring the thread up again just inside the 1,8 point. Repeat stitching sequence as for first round, remembering to thread the last stitch under the first of that round as before (figure 6c).

*Star 1*

This star is stitched in DG, two rounds of stitches being worked.

Stitch a 5 mm gold cup sequin in the central space, holding this in place with a Victorian Gold seed bead. Before fastening the thread off securely at the back, use the needle to adjust the straight stitches so that the sequin can be slipped under the embroidery to peep through.

*Stars 2, 11 and 22*

Work the star outline in DG as for the previous star. Attach a 5 mm

red cup sequin in the centre,
holding this in place with a red
seed bead. Sew one Old Gold seed
bead in each of the spaces
between the points of the star in
the positions indicated on figure 4.

### Star 3

As before, stitch this star in DG.
Use a tiny (3 or 4 mm) cup or flat
gold sequin secured with a
Victorian Gold seed bead. Sew
one petite Old Gold seed bead in
the spaces between the points of
the star. Note that this star sits
close to Star 2 and the beads
placed in the spaces may be very
close together.

### Stars 5, 17 and 21

Stitch the stars in DG, again
stitching two rounds. A Victorian
Gold bead holds a 5 or 6 mm gold
cup sequin in place in the centre.
Stitch one Old Gold seed bead in
the spaces between the points.

### Stars 6 and 9

These stars are stitched with DS,
and two rounds are worked. Stitch
one 5 or 6 mm green cup sequin
in the centre with an emerald seed
bead.

### Star 8

Stitch the star in two rounds of DS. A 5 or 6 mm red cup sequin is held in place with a red seed bead.

### Stars 10 and 19

One round only in DG is stitched for these stars, which have no beading.

### Star 13

Two rounds are stitched in DG.

### Star 14

Stitch two rounds with G. Sew a 6 mm red cup sequin with a 3 mm gold pearl bead in the centre, and Antique Red seed beads in the spaces between the points.

### Star 26

Stitch two rounds in DS. Stitch a 5 or 6 mm silver cup sequin in the centre, held in place by a red seed bead.

### Star 27

Stitch two rounds in DS. Stitch a 4 or 5 mm green cup sequin in the centre with an emerald seed bead. A silver Delica seed bead is stitched in each of the spaces between the points.

## FLY STITCH STAR

### Star 18

This star is made up of five fly stitches, stems being inserted at the centre point of the star.

Before beginning to stitch this star it is helpful to add marks for the centre point and inner angles between the points to the existing markers.

Using G, stitch the ears of the first fly from two adjacent points of the star (1 and 2 in figure 7a). Bring the thread for the anchor stitch up at the inner angle between these points (3) and insert it at the centre of the star (4).

The next stitch will start from the next (5) and previous (1) points, with the anchor arising at 6 and ending in the centre (figure 7b). Continue stitching in this manner until all points have been completed (figure 7c).

Straight stitches are then sewn from just inside each point to the centre. This completes the star (figure 7d).

This creates a more delicate star than those stitched previously. Others like it could be used as fill-ins later in the stitching or, like many decorations on family Christmas trees, can be kept as a one-off and allowed to be a surprise element.

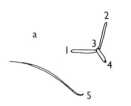

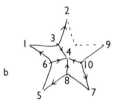

Figure 7: Fly stitch star

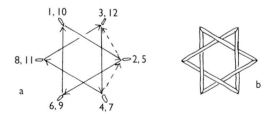

Figure 8: Six-point star

## Basic six-point star

This star is worked in a similar way to the basic five-point star with just one additional point.

As for the five-point star, commence by bringing the thread up at 1 and work around in sequence to 11 (figure 8a). As before, pass the thread under the stitch 1 to 2 before inserting at 12 (figure 8b).

### Star 20

Stitch this star in DS, completing two rounds. As the centre space is quite large, stitch a combination of a 10 mm flat silver sequin, an 8 mm flat red sequin and a 6 mm silver cup sequin in place with a red seed bead. Stitch a 3 mm white pearl bead in each of the spaces between the points.

### Star 24

Stitch two rounds in DG. A 4 or 5 mm gold cup sequin is held in the centre by a Victorian Gold seed bead. Old Gold petite seed beads are stitched in the spaces between the points.

## Basic eight-point star

Work long straight stitches in the order shown in figure 9a, noting that for this star, instead of missing one point as for five-point and six-point stars, two spaces are missed between the top stitches (e.g. 1 to 2), and the thread is taken back two spaces for the underneath stitch (2 to 3). For the final stitch, bring needle up at 15, pass it under stitches 1 to 2, and 3 to 4, then bring it down at 16.

Your finished star should look like the star in figure 9b where all stitches are interwoven.

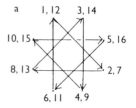

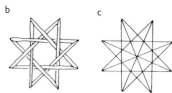

Figure 9: Eight-point star

*Star 15*

Stitch star as above using DS. Then stitch four long straight stitches between opposite points as shown in figure 9c. Stitches should cross at the middle point of the star.

Attach a 6 mm silver cup sequin to the centre of the star with a Christmas Green seed bead. Stitch a 3 mm white pearl bead in each of the spaces between the points.

### LAZY DAISY STAR

*Stars 4, 16 and 25*

Mark the central point of the star on the silk foundation, using the existing tacked markers for reference.

Using DR, stitch six detached chain around this central point to form a lazy daisy (figure 10a). Change to DS and stitch six straight stitches to form spokes between the petals—start each stitch close to the centre and between each pair of petals, end it midway between the ends of the petals (figure 10b). Next, continuing with the silver thread, stitch one straight stitch inside each petal as a highlight. Start just inside the tip and end close to the origin of the stitch at the centre (figure 10c).

Finish the star by sewing a 3 mm silver pearl bead in the centre.

### Star 7

The lazy daisy for this star is worked in 1 strand of D5269. The spokes and highlights are stitched in DS and a 3 mm silver pearl bead is stitched in the centre.

### Star 12

This star is stitched completely in DG. A 3 mm gold pearl bead is stitched in the centre. Sew one Old Gold seed bead to the tip of each spoke, securing the thread at the back after each bead is attached. It is important to do this due to the distance the thread travels between each bead.

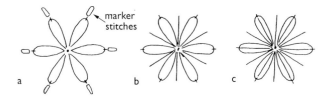

*Figure 10: Lazy daisy star*

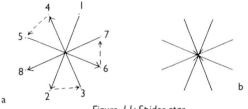

Figure 11: Spider star

## SPIDER STAR

This is a simple, unembellished star created by working four long straight stitches caught at the centre by a small cross-stitch. To create the four straight stitches, stitch in the order shown in figure 11a. Once these have been stitched, bring the needle up close to the centre and between two of the spokes. Take it over all the threads at the centre and down in the opposite space. To complete the cross, skip one space, bring the needle up in the next and down in the space opposite as before (figure 11b). Secure the thread firmly at the back.

This is a useful star to use as a fill-in and can look particularly pretty kept small and stitched in machine metallic embroidery thread.

### Star 23

Stitch as above in DS.

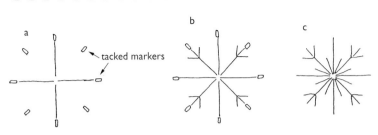

*Figure 12: Snowflake A*

### Snowflake A

Working within the tacked markers, and using DS, stitch a cross with four straight stitches, each stitch beginning at the outside and ending in the centre (figure 12a).

Add four winged spokes: working from the outside, stitch one short straight stitch (about one-third the length of the finished arm) and one long-tailed fly stitch. Take the tail of the fly to the centre of the snowflake (figure 12b).

Finally, add straight stitches between each spoke, making these about half the length of the others (figure 12c).

Stitch one petite white seed bead at the end of the shorter spokes.

### Snowflake B

This snowflake is worked in DG and is stitched in fly stitch.

Starting at the outer end of one spoke, stitch one straight stitch ending about a quarter of the way down the spoke. Now stitch a fly stitch at the base of this, inserting the anchor stitch halfway down the spoke. Stitch a second fly stitch with the anchor ending three-quarters of the way down, and a third fly stitch with its anchor inserting at the centre of the snowflake (figure 13a).

Repeat for the remaining seven spokes, building the shape up from a cross to the completed snowflake (figures 13b and 13c).

a

b

c

*Figure 13: Snowflake B*

Photocopy figure 14 at 167%. Use the tissue paper method to transfer the detailed outline of the heart, gingerbread man, snowman, the two birds and the angel decorations (but not the balls or bells) from figure 14 to the foundation shape. Use small stitches and, after anchoring your thread, stitch only through the silk. Smooth off the fabric if it puckers when the tissue paper is removed.

Unless stated otherwise, all embroidery is done using one strand of the specified thread in a size 10 crewel needle.

## HEART

Outline the shape in split backstitch through all layers using RJ255. Make your stitches as small as possible in order to achieve an accurate shape (figure 15a). Embroider the heart in padded satin stitch.

Continuing with the red thread, fill in the shape with satin stitch. Keep the stitches close to and inside the split backstitch outline (figure 15b). Add one strand of K003 to the needle and complete another layer of satin stitch, this time working at right angles to the previous layer and taking the stitches over the split backstitch (figure 15c).

A row of stem stitch in G is now worked around the heart. Begin this at the indent on the top of the heart and stitch around and as close as possible to the outer edge of the motif (figure 15d).

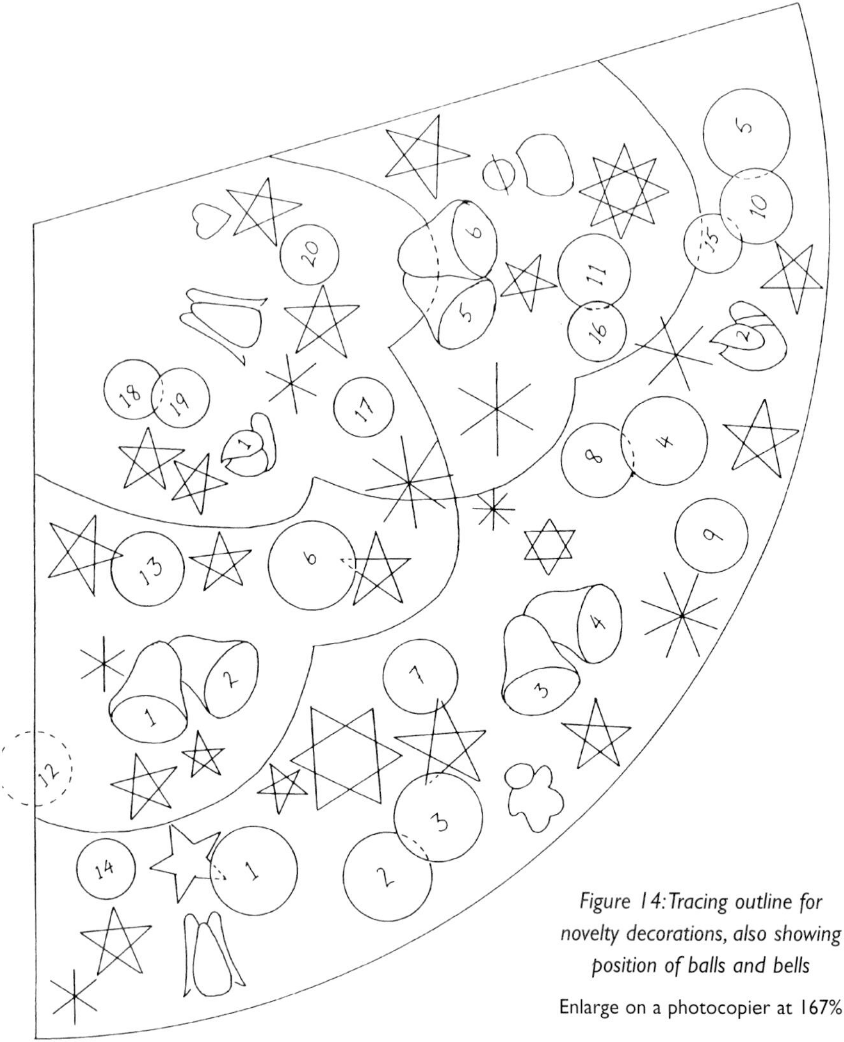

*Figure 14: Tracing outline for novelty decorations, also showing position of balls and bells*

Enlarge on a photocopier at 167%

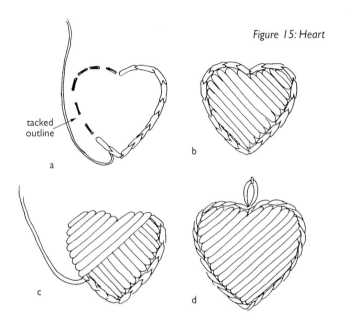

*Figure 15: Heart*

tacked
outline

a

b

c

d

Before ending off, stitch one detached chain at the top for the hanging loop. Make sure that it points towards the apex of the tree.

## GINGERBREAD MAN

Outline the entire head, then the body, with small tacking stitches. Using one strand of D436, work one row of split backstitch along the tacked outline of the head and body.

Work the head and body separately in padded satin stitch, as for the heart. Make sure that the direction of stitches is consistent from the head to the body (figure 16).

Stitch one fly stitch in RJ255 for the mouth. The eyes and buttons are French knots of one wrap in RJ175.

Beginning at the top of the head, work one row of stem stitch in G around and as close as possible to the outer edge of the

*Figure 16: Gingerbread man*

motif. Before ending off, stitch one detached chain at the top of the head for the hanging loop.

## SNOWMAN

Outline the head and the body separately in split backstitch using RJ96. Complete the head and body shapes in padded satin stitch (figure 17a). Work the first layer

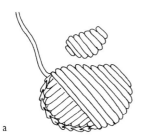

a

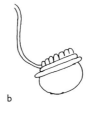

b

c

d

e

*Figure 17: Snowman*

with RJ96. Add one strand of K032 for the second layer.

Outline the hat in split backstitch using RJ29. Fill with padded satin stitch. As before, keep the first layer inside the outline, but with stitches running from the top to the bottom of the crown. Add one strand of K019 to the needle before stitching the top layer which runs horizontally across the hat (figure 17b). The brim is formed by one or two long straight stitches.

For the scarf, work two rows of alternating chain stitch in the neck space between the head and body, using RJ255 and RJ152. Stitch a further two rows for the loose ends of the scarf (figure17c). Create a fringe at each end of the scarf by stitching three tiny straight stitches running out from the end of the last chain stitch. Keeping both threads in the needle, work two small straight stitches to form the knot at the edge of the neck.

Using one thread each of D436 and K027, make three long straight stitches for the broomstick (figure 17d). Begin each stitch at the point where the bristles will meet the handle, ending at a point towards the base of the body (figure17e)—stitching in this direction will help to prevent distortion of the satin stitches. Using the same threads, couch in place with three stitches equally placed along the length of the handle, as shown in figure 17d.

The brush bristles are made from five straight stitches radiating slightly from the top end of the broomstick. When completed, stitch three satin stitches across the base of the brush.

Create the snowman's mouth by working one fly stitch in RJ255.

Work the eyes and buttons in single-wrap French knots in RJ29.

Beginning at the top of the head, work one row of stem stitch in S around and as close as possible to the outer edge of snowman (not the broom). Before

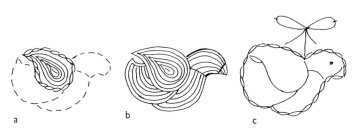

*Figure 18: Bird 1*

ending off, stitch one detached chain at the top of the head for the hanging loop.

## BIRD 1

Beginning at the tip, outline the shape of the wing with tiny stem stitches in RJ152. Stitch a second row close to the first following the same direction and line. Continue in this manner until the wing shape is completely filled with rows of stem stitch. The pattern created by the lines of stitches is shown in figure 18a.

Using RJ788, outline the shape of head in stem stitch, working from the edge of the wing, across the base of the beak (the beak does not appear in the tracing diagram, figure 14) to where it meets the breast. As with the wing, completely fill the head area with rows of tiny stem stitches. Start each row at the wing and work towards the beak as shown in figure 18b.

The breast (RJ44) and tail (RJ788) are worked in the same manner as the wing and head.

Refer to figure 18b to determine the direction of the rows of stem stitch.

The beak is worked in satin stitch with RJ44.

A two-wrap French knot in RJ29 creates the eye.

To finish, begin at the top of the neck and work one row of stem stitch in G around and as close as possible to the outer edge of the bird. Continuing with G, work three straight stitches and two detached chain stitches to create the tie (figure 18c).

## BIRD 2

Like Bird 1, the wing, head and body are all stitched in rows of stem stitch. Figure 19 shows the direction of the lines to be

*Figure 19: Bird 2*

followed. Start with the wing, using RJ181.

Next, outline the shape of the head in RJ113, working from the wing at the back to where it meets the collar at the front. Fill the head area with stem stitch, starting each row at the beak and working back towards the collar.

The body and tail are worked in RJ113.

Work the collar in satin stitch using RJ788 in the direction shown in figure 19. This row of stitches should fill the gap between the head and body.

The beak and eye as well as the finishing are the same as for Bird 1.

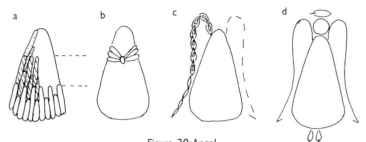

*Figure 20: Angel*

## ANGELS

Outline the dress in split backstitch using RJ96, then thread the needle with one strand of RJ96 and K032.

Completely fill in the shape of the dress with three rows of long and short stitch. Starting at the bottom, with the long stitches reaching about one-third of the way up, work one row. Stitches along the edge should just cover the outlining stitches (note that the outlining stitches are not shown in figure 20a).

Work a further two rows of long and short stitch, reducing the number of stitches per row as the shape narrows. To achieve a smooth finish, in the second and following rows, insert the needle into the end of the stitch below it. This will split the thread and prevent a hollow forming between the rows. Make sure that the direction of the stitches flows towards the neck as shown. Fill in the remaining space at the neck with a few straight stitches.

Work the arms and hands with three fly stitches (figure 20b), again using both RJ96 and K032. Begin the first stitch about one-quarter of the way down from the top, finishing with a tiny anchor stitch further down along the centre line of the dress. Start each stitch just below the previous one but stitch all anchoring stitches at the same point. This build up of stitches creates the hands.

If any background fabric shows through the long and short stitches after the hands have been stitched, cover the space with one or two straight stitches.

The wings are stitched in S. Start at the top of one wing where it is attached to the body. Stitch one row of tiny chain stitches along the outer edge to about two-thirds the way down, then change to stem stitch and complete stitching to the end of the wing (figure 20c). End this thread off. Work a further three or four rows in the same manner until the shape is filled.

Complete the second wing in the same manner.

Work two detached chain stitches in RJ96 at the bottom of the dress to create the feet.

**Finishing** This is not done until you get to layer 4. Attach a 4 mm pearl bead for the head using invisible thread. End off firmly so that the pearl sits close to the fabric. Stitch one detached chain stitch in DG running across the top of the head for the halo.

# Layer 3: Balls and bells

The balls and bells are worked as individual elements and then attached to the foundation.

## BALLS

1. The foundation shapes for the balls are cut from a heavyweight paper such as cartridge or 110 gsm office paper. You will need six large, seven medium and seven small circles. Cut as accurately as possible keeping the edges smooth. If you do not have access to a small compass from a geometry set, trace the shapes from figure 21.

2. Cut a circle of silk to cover the paper circle, adding a seam allowance all round of about 6 mm (¼ in). To prevent excess fraying, cut with pinking shears. Make sure the seam allowance is within the zigzag edge (figure 22a).

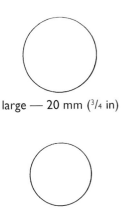

large — 20 mm (³/₄ in)

medium — 17 mm (¹¹/₁₆ in)

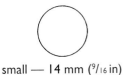

small — 14 mm (⁹/₁₆ in)

*Figure 21: Tracing outlines for ball foundations*

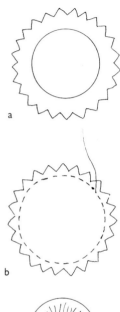

*Figure 22: Covering ball foundation*

**3.** With right side of silk facing, and starting with a knot, stitch a row of very small gathering stitches around the entire outside edge, about 2 mm in, finishing one or two stitches past the knot (figure 22b). Keeping your stitches small will give a better result in the next step.

**4.** Place foundation shape on the wrong side of the silk, pull gathering stitches up firmly so that the shape is covered and the edges are smooth (figure 22c). I find it easiest to do this by stabilising the silk and paper shape on the table with my left index finger while pulling the thread up with my right hand. Adjust gathers evenly around the circumference and secure the end of the thread.

**5.** Complete embroidery and beading for each ball as described below. Note that the finishing off of each ball is done after it has been appliquéd to the tree, as described on page 63.

*Ball 1*

Cover a 20 mm (¾ inch) shape with red silk. Mark the lines of the bands around the ball onto the front of the silk (figure 23a). A fabric-marking pen can be used, but dressmaking carbon paper gives a better result. Using one strand of R44, work one row of tiny stem stitches along the top line. Continuing with the same

thread, fill the space between the second and third lines with double buttonhole stitch (figure 23b).

The zigzags are worked by stitching three straight stitches evenly spaced across the ball from bottom to top and left to right, then returning with three stitches from bottom to top, right to left. Sew one Old Gold bead in the spaces adjacent to the central band as shown.

**Finishing** Following application to the tree, DG thread is couched around the shape with G. A detached chain stitch at the top makes a tiny hanging loop. A 3 mm gold pearl bead is stitched at the base at this later stage.

a  b

*Figure 23: Ball 1*

### Ball 2

Cover a 20 mm (¾ inch) shape with yellow silk. Mark the centre and six points spaced evenly around the circumference of the circle (figure 24a). Working around the centre point, and sewing in a stab stitch manner through all layers, work a lazy daisy in DG. Continuing with the same thread, stitch a second petal inside the previous ones, taking the anchoring stitch of this over both stitches and insert at the outer

edge of the daisy (figure 24b).

Sew a 3 mm gold pearl bead in the centre of the motif and red seed beads in the spaces between each of the petals.

**Finishing** The ball is outlined in gold and a 3 mm gold pearl bead is attached to the bottom once it has been attached to the tree.

### Ball 3

Cover a 20 mm (¾ inch) shape with bottle green silk. Mark six points spaced evenly around the

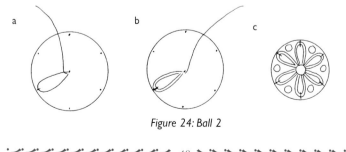

*Figure 24: Ball 2*

*Figure 25: Ball 3*

circumference of the circle. Stitch a six-point star in DG, then take a small stitch to catch threads at intersections as shown in figure 25. Sew a combination of three sequins—a 10 mm flat gold, an 8 mm flat red and a 6 mm cup gold—and a red seed bead in the centre.

**Finishing** This ball will be outlined in gold and have a 3 mm gold pearl bead at its base.

*Ball 4*

Cover a 20 mm (¾ inch) shape with golden green silk. Work a circle of small chain stitches a little way in from the outside edge in D581r. Sew a lazy daisy in the centre using DR, making each petal double as for Ball 2. With DG, work a straight-stitch highlight inside each petal, running from the centre to the inner tip of each. Sew a 3 mm gold pearl bead in the centre and a petite old gold bead between the petals (figure 26).

**Finishing** This ball will be outlined in gold and have a 3 mm gold pearl bead at its base.

*Figure 26: Ball 4*

## Ball 5

## Ball 6

Cover a 20 mm (¾ inch) shape with red silk. Work a lazy daisy with eight petals with DG. Sew a 3 mm gold pearl bead in the centre and Old Gold seed beads in the spaces between the petals (figure 27).

**Finishing** This ball will be outlined in gold and have a 3 mm gold pearl bead at its base.

Cover a 20 mm (¾ inch) shape with royal blue silk. Use the DMC silver thread to create a lattice of 3 x 3 threads (figure 28a). Stitch a tiny 4-petalled lazy daisy in the centre of each square, and portions of a daisy in the spaces at the sides

*Figure 27: Ball 5*

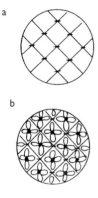

*Figure 28: Ball 6*

with R. Stitch a French knot (RJ255, 1 thread, 2 wraps) in the centre of each daisy (figure 28b).

**Finishing** This ball will be outlined in silver and have a 3 mm pearl at its base.

a

b

Figure 29: Ball 7

### Ball 7

Cover a 17 mm ($^{11}/_{16}$ inch) shape with golden green silk. Sew a 3 mm gold pearl bead to the centre. Sew on four Victorian Gold bugle beads, starting close to the central bead and ending at the outer edge of the ball so that they form a cross (figure 29a). Sew red bugle beads in the spaces between to form another cross (figure 29b).

**Finishing** This ball will be outlined in gold and have a 3 mm gold pearl bead at its base.

### Ball 8

Cover a 17 mm ($^{11}/_{16}$ inch) shape with bottle green silk. Make a cross on the front of the ball with KR002 (figure 30a), bringing the thread up on the very edge of the covered shape and leaving an end of about 1 cm hanging at the back. Make sure the ribbon has

a

b

c

*Figure 30: Ball 8*

30b). Start each stitch by catching the ribbon where it crosses at the centre. Sew a 6 mm gold cup sequin and red seed bead in the centre and an Old Gold seed bead inside and toward the end of each petal (figure 30c).

**Finishing** This ball will be outlined in gold and have a 3 mm gold pearl bead at its base.

*Ball 9*

not twisted before inserting it at a point directly opposite, again on the edge. Carry this across at the back before making another stitch at right angles to the first. Cut the ribbon off, leaving a 1 cm (⅜ inch) end at the back. These two ends can be stitched down during subsequent stitching.

A detached chain stitch in DG is placed in each quarter (figure

Cover a 17 mm (¹¹⁄₁₆ inch) shape with royal blue silk. Mark five points equally around the circle and close to the edge. Stitch a basic five-point star between these points (figure 31a), then a straight stitch from each point to the centre (figure 31b). Finally, sew straight stitches to join all the points around the outside (figure

31c). A 5 mm or smaller silver sequin and royal blue seed bead is stitched in the centre of the star.

**Finishing** This ball will be outlined in silver and have a 3 mm silver pearl bead at its base.

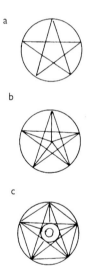

a

b

c

*Figure 31: Ball 9*

Cover a 17 mm ($^{11}/_{16}$ inch) shape with white silk. Work a lazy daisy with six petals with DG. Stitch another lazy daisy stitch inside each petal as for Ball 4. Sew a 3 mm gold pearl bead in the centre and petite white seed beads in the spaces between the petals (figure 32).

**Finishing** This ball will be outlined in gold and have a 3 mm gold pearl bead at its base.

*Figure 32: Ball 10*

## Ball 11

## Ball 12

Cover a 17 mm (¹¹⁄₁₆ inch) shape with turquoise silk. Stitch a 3 mm gold pearl bead in the centre. Bringing the needle up next to this bead, sew four Victorian Gold bugle beads around it to form a cross. Sew four more of these bugle beads in the spaces between. Sew a red silver-lined Delica bead in the spaces between the bugle beads close to the central bead (figure 33).

**Finishing** This ball will be outlined in gold and have a 3 mm gold pearl bead at its base.

Cover a 17 mm (¹¹⁄₁₆ inch) shape with yellow silk. Stitch a lazy daisy with eight petals and straight stitch highlights in DG. Stitch a 5 mm gold cup sequin with an Old Gold seed bead in the centre and Christmas Green seed beads around the edge in the spaces between the petals (figure 34).

**Finishing** This ball is attached to the foundation after the side seam has been stitched. Outline in gold and stitch a 3 mm gold pearl bead on the seam at its base.

*Figure 33: Ball 11*

*Figure 34: Ball 12*

### Ball 13

### Ball 14

Cover a 17 mm (¹¹⁄₁₆ inch) shape with red silk. Make a cross on the front of the ball with KR102. Work a detached chain stitch in DG in each quarter. Sew a 6 mm gold cup sequin and red seed bead in the centre, and an Old Gold seed bead inside and toward the centre of each petal (figure 35).

**Finishing** This ball will be outlined in gold and have a 3 mm gold pearl bead at its base.

Cover a 14 mm (⁹⁄₁₆ inch) shape with royal blue silk. Stitch a ring of chain stitches in DG about 2 mm in from the edge. Stitch a 5 mm cup gold sequin and a Victorian Gold seed bead in the centre (figure 36).

**Finishing** This ball will be outlined in gold and have a 2 mm gold pearl bead at its base.

Figure 36: Ball 14

Figure 35: Ball 13

## Ball 15

Cover a 14 mm (%₁₆ inch) shape with yellow silk. Stitch a lazy daisy with five petals in DG. Sew an Old Gold seed bead in the centre and four more between the petals close to the centre (figure 37).

**Finishing** This ball will be outlined in gold and have a 2 mm gold pearl bead at its base.

## Ball 16

Cover a 14 mm (%₁₆ inch) shape with red silk. Stitch a six-point star in DG. A combination of a 6 mm flat gold sequin, 5 mm red cup sequin and red seed bead is sewn in the centre. Old Gold petite seed beads are stitched in the spaces between the points (figure 38).

**Finishing** This ball will be outlined in gold and have a 2 mm gold pearl bead at its base.

*Figure 37: Ball 15*

*Figure 38: Ball 16*

## Ball 17

Cover a 14 mm (⁹⁄₁₆ inch) shape with red silk. Stitch a lazy daisy with five petals in DG. Sew a 5 mm gold sequin with a red seed bead in the centre. Old Gold petite seed beads are stitched between the petals close to the edge (figure 39).

**Finishing** This ball will be outlined in gold and have a 2 mm gold pearl bead at its base.

*Figure 39: Ball 17*

## Ball 18

Cover a 14 mm (⁹⁄₁₆ inch) shape with bottle green silk. Using two strands of RJ44, stitch a six-point star of two rounds. Stitch a 5 mm gold cup sequin with an Old Gold seed bead in the centre (figure 40).

**Finishing** This ball will be outlined in gold and have a 2 mm gold pearl bead at its base.

*Figure 40: Ball 18*

## Ball 19

Cover a 14 mm (%₁₆ inch) shape with white silk. Work a lazy daisy with five petals in DG. Sew a red seed bead in the centre. Christmas Green seed beads are stitched between the petals close to the central bead (figure 41).

**Finishing** This ball will be outlined in gold and have a 2 mm gold pearl bead at its base.

*Figure 41: Ball 19*

## Ball 20

Cover a 14 mm (%₁₆ inch) shape with golden green silk. Work a ring of feather stitches close to the edge of the shape in DG. Stitch a 5 mm or smaller gold sequin and a Victorian Gold seed bead in the centre (figure 42).

**Finishing** This ball will be outlined in gold and have a 2 mm gold pearl bead at its base.

*Figure 42: Ball 20*

## BELLS

1. Cut out six bell shapes from the pattern in figure 43a and cover, following steps 1–4 for balls on page 45. Before cutting thread after gathering and securing, lace the raw edges together along the length of the bell to ensure a snug fit along the concave sides (figure 43b).

2. Complete all embroidery and beading referring to instructions for specific bells. Tongues and bows are added after application to tree.

### Bell 1

Cover bell shape with burgundy silk. With a light-coloured pencil or fabric-marking pen, draw the mouth of the bell on the silk.

Outline the mouth in stem stitch using DG: starting on the left side, work one row across the top through all layers. When you reach the right-hand side, continue along the bottom, stitching on the very edge of the shape. To do this you will need to hold the covered shape between your thumb and index finger so that the edge is uppermost. Catch only the fabric in your needle. When your stitches meet up on the left-hand side, make one stitch over the first of the initial row and work another row of stem stitches above and hard up against the first. You will now have two rows of stem stitching at the front of the bell mouth, and one at the back.

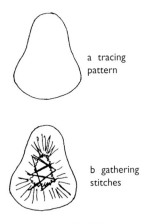

a tracing pattern

b gathering stitches

*Figure 43: Bell*

*Figure 44: Bell I*

*Bell 2*

Cover bell shape with golden green silk. As with Bell 1, outline the mouth of the bell with stem stitch in DG, sewing two rows at the front and one at the back.

Still using DG, work another row of stem stitch about 3 mm (⅛ inch) above the rim.

Using the same thread, work one row of chain stitch above and close to the previous embroidery. Finish the band with another row of stem stitch (figure 44).

Starting at the top of the bell and using G, stitch one row of tiny chain stitches down the centre to the top of the band. Return to the same point at the top and stitch another row close to the first but curving slightly to follow the contour of the bell. Repeat three or four times or until you have filled the top with stripes of chain stitching.

*Figure 45: Bell 2*

Use DR to create a row of zigzags in straight stitch in the space between the rows of stem stitch.

Work three rows of vertical fly stitches in G, running up from the band to meet at the top of the bell. Stitch the centre row first. Start by working one small straight stitch followed by a series of about four fly stitches until you reach the top (figure 45). Note that the size of the stitches reduces as they reach the top.

Repeat either side of the centre row, making sure that the fly stitches join up with those they sit beside in the centre and reach the outer edges of the bell. This will give a complete filling to the top area of the bell.

*Figure 46: Bell 3*

above the rim (figure 46).

Work three rows of vertical fly stitch in G, running up from the band and meeting at the centre top, as for Bell 2.

### Bell 3

Cover bell shape with red silk. As before, outline the mouth of the bell with stem stitch in DG, sewing two rows at the front and one at the back. Stem stitch another row about 3 mm (⅛ inch)

*Figure 47: Bell 4*

## Bell 4

Cover bell shape with white silk.
Outline the mouth of the bell
with stem stitch in DR, working
two rows at the front and one at
the back. Complete the band with
one row of chain stitch in DG and
one row of stem stitch in DR.

Fill the top of the bell with
trellis couching worked in R
(figure 47).

## Bell 5

Cover bell shape with white silk.
Using B as the passing thread,
couch KB033 around the mouth
of the bell, two rows at the front
and one along the back edge.
Couch another row about 3 mm
(⅛ inch) above the rim, making

*Figure 48: Bell 5*

sure that this follows the curve of
the mouth. (The braid can simply
be laid along the top of the silk
for couching. As it is very soft, the
ends can be folded over the edges
of the silk and stitched down on
the back with RJ126 before using
this to stitch the zigzag.)

Using RJ126, stitch a row of
straight-stitch zigzags in the band
space, then stitch a one-wrap
French knot in the same thread in
the zigzag spaces (figure 48).

Using B, fill the top of the bell
with tiny star stitches.

*Figure 49: Bell 6*

*Bell 6*

Cover bell shape with royal blue silk. Use DS to outline the mouth of the bell with stem stitch, again working two rows at the front and one at the back. Work another row of stem stitch about 2 mm (¹⁄₁₆ inch) above the last row.

Fill the top of the bell with trellis couching stitched in DS (figure 49).

## ATTACHING BALLS AND BELLS TO FOUNDATION

Begin by attaching a length of contrasting thread to the apex of the foundation shape. Cut this so that it is 5–8 centimetres (2–3 inches) longer than the shape. This will act as a plumbline, a guide for ensuring balls, bells and other decorations hang at an appropriate angle when the tree is finally assembled.

Use figure 14 as a guide to placement of the ball and bells.

### BALLS

1. Where balls overlap, e.g. balls 2 and 3, attach the bottom one first.

2. Using a flat surface, position the ball in the appropriate place on the foundation shape. Hold the plumbline over the ball so that the thread passes over its centre.

Reposition the ball so that its top and bottom (if this is defined in the embroidery) are aligned with the thread and hold in place with a pin.

This technique is also used for appropriate placement of hanging loops on the top and beads attached to the bottom of balls.

3. Stitch to the foundation fabric using small slipstitches in a sewing thread matching the foundation fabric.

4. Outline the outer edge of balls with couching, using DG or DS as the laid thread depending on the colour of the threads used within each ball, and as specified in the finishing directions for that ball. Use G or S to stitch it in place.

Start and finish at the top of each ball. Bring the laid thread up at the top of the ball—A in figure 50a. Use the plumbline thread to determine the

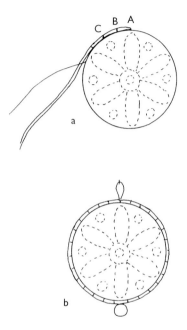

*Figure 50: Attaching a ball*

position of A. Holding the laid thread against the edge of the ball, bring the working thread (G or S) up at B, about 3 mm (⅛ inch) along from A. Insert the needle between the laid thread and the edge of the ball directly opposite B. This should create a tiny stitch sitting at right angles to the laid thread.

Bring the needle up again about 3 mm (about ⅛ inch) further along at C, and make another stitch across the laid thread as before.

Continue in this way until the entire circumference of the ball has been outlined.

Take the laid thread to the back of the foundation at A and secure.

Bring the working thread up at A and make one small detached chain stitch, about 3 mm (⅛ inch) long, to form the hanging loop (figure 50b). Fasten off.

Stitch the pearl bead (see finishing instructions for each ball for colour) at the bottom of the ball, directly opposite the hanging loop. The pearl bead,

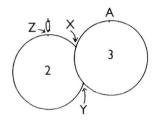

Figure 51: Overlapping balls

hanging loop and apex of the tree should all fall along an imaginary straight line.

5. Where the design specifies overlapping balls, outline the ball sitting at the back first.

Bring the laid thread up at X and couch around to Y. Take laid thread down at Y and bring it up at A, ready to outline the upper ball. With the working thread, stitch a detached chain at the top (Z) of the lower ball. Outline top ball as before. Stitch pearl beads to base of each ball.

## BELLS

Refer to figure 14 for placement. Note that in each pair of bells, one overlaps the other.

1. Stitch in place, taking care that the slipstitches are not visible as the bells are not outlined.

2. Bell tongues: the tongues of bells 1, 2, 3 and 4 are worked in Kreinik 2 mm (¹⁄₁₆ inch) ribbon 002 (Gold), finished with a 3 mm gold pearl bead. The tongues of bells 5 and 6 are worked in Kreinik 2 mm (¹⁄₁₆ inch) ribbon 001 (Silver), finished with a 3 mm silver pearl bead.

Use a no. 7 crewel needle and keep the ribbon flat when stitching. Leaving a short tail on the back of the foundation, bring ribbon up inside the mouth of the bell about two-thirds of the way along the front edge (figure 52a). Insert and pull through to back of work at the bottom back edge

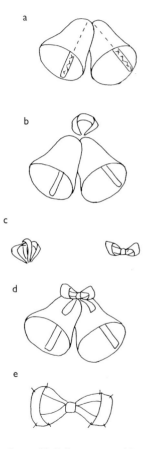

*Figure 52: Bell tongues and bows*

of bell mouth. Make sure the tongue lies as if it was attached to the top of the bell.

Take ribbon across the back and stitch tongue of second bell in same way.

Cut ribbon, leaving an end of about 15 mm (⅝ inch). Stitch down to secure with sewing thread.

3. All bows are stitched with KR102.

Bring ribbon up a little above the top of the pair of bells, leaving a short tail at the back of the work. Insert close to this point and pull ribbon down, leaving a loop (figure 52b) on the right side of the work about 15 mm (⁹⁄₁₆ inch) high— just large enough to fit around the tip of your little finger.

Bring the ribbon up again just below the loop and insert just above, allowing the stitch made to catch and flatten the loop midway making two smaller loops (figure 52c).

Decide where you would like the ribbon ends to fall in relation to the bells and bring the needle up at this point. Insert at the base of the bow (figure 52d).

Stitch the other end in the same way. Leave ends of ribbon at back.

Using invisible thread, make small stitches through the edges of the loops as shown to shape and flatten the bow (figure 52e).

Stitch down loose ends on back of work.

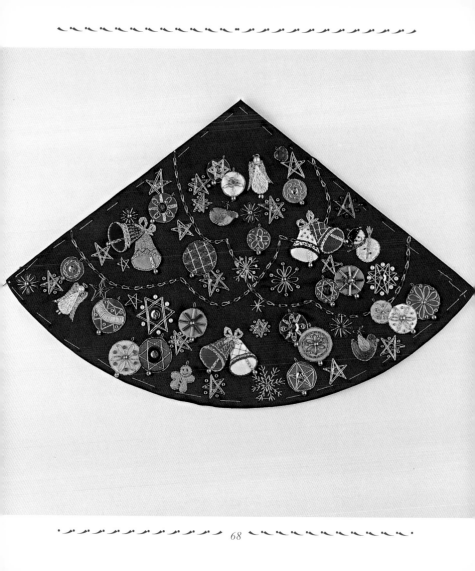

# Layer 4: Beading and fill-ins

The solid lines on Figure 53 indicate the placement of the embellishments worked in this final layer.

### FINISHING ANGELS, BALLS, BELLS, STARS AND SNOWFLAKES

1. Attach the 4 mm white pearl beads to create the heads of the angels. Stitch the halos above using DG.

2. Attach the gold or silver pearl beads to the bases of all balls.

3. Attach gold or silver pearl beads to the end of the bell tongues.

4. Complete the beading of all stars and snowflakes—refer to previous instructions for the specific finishing touches for each one. Figure 4 or Figure 53 can be used for clarification of positions.

### CANDLES

Stitch a silver twisted bugle bead in place for the main part of each candle. Use the plumbline to

*Figure 54a: Candle*

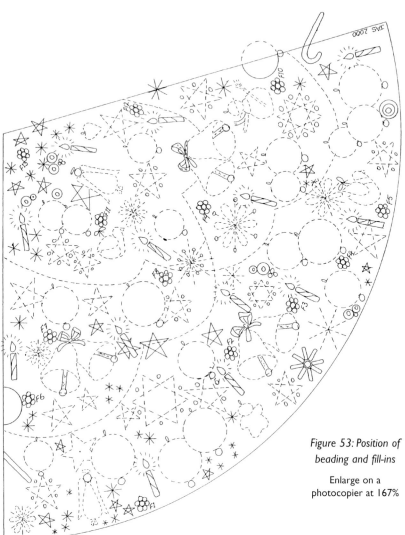

Figure 53: Position of
beading and fill-ins

Enlarge on a
photocopier at 167%

*Figure 54b: Candle*

ensure the bead points towards the apex of the tree.

Stitch five Victorian Gold seed beads at the base of each candle as shown in figure 54a. Bring the threaded needle up about 2 mm (¹⁄₁₆ inch) above the base of the candle and close to its side, thread the five beads on the needle and insert at the opposite side of the base of the candle. Hold the beads in place by making a small stitch between each pair of beads as shown.

Work the flame in satin stitch using DG (figure 54b). Start in the middle with the longest stitch, then working outwards, stitch the two shorter stitches on each side.

Stitch the halo around the flame in G. This is done by working 12–13 tiny straight stitches in a circle radiating out around the flame. In some cases the halo will overlap other embroidery and should be stitched as such. Where the halo falls on the seam line, wait until this part of the seam has been joined before working it.

### BUGLE BEAD STAR

Work the bugle bead star motif shown on figure 53 that sits below bells 2 and 3. Stitch a tiny gold sequin and green seed bead in the centre. Alternate four yellow–gold 6 mm bugle beads with four lime green beads to form an eight–

point star, then stitch Old Gold
seed beads between each bugle.

### BEADED FLOWERS

Work the beaded flower motifs
(F1, F2, etc.) using beads as listed
below. Refer to figure 53 for
placement. Each motif consists of
one central bead surrounded by
6–8 seed beads. Attach the central
bead first. Using backstitch, stitch
each surrounding bead
individually, spacing them evenly
around and touching the central
bead.

* Flowers F1, F2, F4, F7, F9, F10,
  F11 and F13 are worked with a
  red seed bead centre
  surrounded by Old Gold seed
  bead 'petals'.

* F3 and F8 are worked with a
  Christmas Green seed bead
  centre surrounded by crystal
  seed bead 'petals'.

* F5 is worked with a 3 mm
  white pearl bead centre
  surrounded by Ice Blue seed
  bead 'petals'.

* F6 is worked with an Old Gold
  seed bead centre surrounded by
  Victorian Gold seed bead
  'petals'.

* F12 is worked with a Christmas
  Green seed bead centre
  surrounded by silver Delica
  seed bead 'petals'.

## CANDY CANE

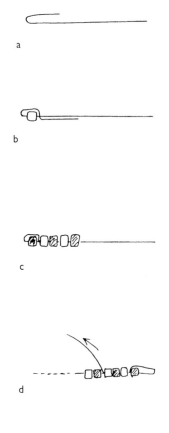

Cut a piece of 34-gauge beading wire approximately 15 cm (6 inches) long. Make a sharp loop 10 mm (⅜ inch) from one end (figure 55a). Thread a Crayon Red seed bead on to the wire and let it sit within the loop.

Squeeze the short end of the wire in so that it fits neatly around the first bead and lies alongside the main length of wire (figure 55b).

Thread on one Crayon White bead so that it fits over both wires and sits on the red bead. Continue threading red and white beads consecutively until you have 12 of each colour on the wire (figure 55c).

Thread a final red bead on the wire, then take the wire back so

*Figure 55: Candy cane*

that it passes over the last red bead and down through the centres of the next four or five beads (figure 55d).

Pull firmly (fine-nosed pliers make this easier) so that all the beads are fairly closely packed on the wire. Pull the wire to the outside and trim off close to where it emerges.

Bend the top of the cane to form the curved handle.

The candy cane is attached to the tree after the side seam has been stitched.

## FILL-IN SEQUINS, STARS AND BEADS

Now that your tree is almost finished, you will find you have a number of gaps, especially towards the top. These spaces can be filled in with a scattering of tiny stars, stitched with a variety of metallic threads; and a scattering of seed beads and sequins, used either alone or in groups; flat-backed sew-on crystals and treasures; and the names of family members. This is an opportunity for you to increase the individuality of your tree.

Use figure 53 as a guide as to how this can be done.

The scattering of stars is stitched in various sizes and styles. Use fine threads for tiny spider stars and star stitches, and to give any larger stars a more delicate appearance. Use S to stitch the three points of the star that is peeping out from behind the angel towards the top of the tree.

The sequins and beads are sewn singly or in combinations and clusters. Keep those towards the top of the tree small so that they do not stand out too far from the surface when the tree is joined. Star sequins make good fillers; use tiny ones at the top, increasing in size towards the bottom. Don't overdo this step, however—too many may detract from your beautiful embroidery.

If you wish to, add a few flat-backed sew-on crystals and Mill Hill Crystal Treasures.

Adding the names of your family members, stitched in fine metallic thread, will contribute to the tree's future as an heirloom; for the same reason, you should find a space for your name or initials, and the year it was made.

Remember to leave spaces along the seam, towards the base, to take Ball 12 and the candy cane.

# Stumpwork star

The tree is crowned with this delicate three-dimensional star.

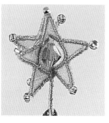

1. Mount the 16 cm (6½ inch) square of gold-coloured fabric in the embroidery hoop and make as taut as possible.

2. Transfer the shape of the star (figure 56) to the fabric. Trace the star onto a piece of paper small enough to fit under the embroidery ring. Place this on a jar lid or similar round, flat-topped object that will fit within the hoop under the fabric. This is to provide a firm surface on which to support the fabric while tracing the star.

3. Couch the paper-covered wire to the fabric, bending it to follow the star shape as you stitch. Use eyebrow tweezers to achieve the sharp bends at the points of the star.

Starting about 5 cm (2 inches) in from the end of the wire, make your first bend midway between the two points closest to the edge of the hoop. Make one stitch to hold this bend in place. Bend the wire to fit neatly around the first point, stitch in place (figure 57a).

*Figure 56: Tracing outline for stumpwork star*

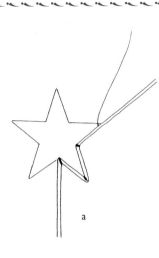

a

Continue couching in this way until the wire is formed into the shape of the star. Do not cut the thread or wire yet.

4. Place the hoop on the support used in step 2. Hold a round pencil on its flat end in the centre of the star and gently bend the wire around it to shape a central ring (figure 57b).

5. Couch in place, bringing the thread up between the two wires where they meet and down inside the ring.

6. Cut the wire close to the end of the ring and make sure it is secured firmly with the couching thread.

7. Oversew around the outer edge of the star with D729 or R45, starting with a waste knot. As the finished star will be viewed from both sides, make sure your stitches

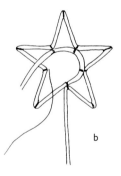

b

*Figure 57: Couching the wire shape*

(a) enclose the long stitches on the back;

(b) catch enough fabric to attach the wire to the fabric;

(c) are close enough to prevent the wire showing through.

**8.** Oversew the ring, taking the thread over both wires where these meet. When you reach the end of the ring, make sure the end of the wire is covered and secure. End off by tying the thread (do not cut it off) securely to the top of the stalk.

*Figure 58: Oversewing the star*

**9.** Make a second star in the same manner.

**10.** Remove the fabric from the hoop and cut around each star, taking care not to snip the overcasting stitch. Trim close to the stitching—you are aiming to get as smooth an edge as possible!

**11.** Cut the fabric from the centre ring and trim close to stitching.

**12.** Using G, add highlights to the edge of each star by adding another layer of stitches. This time space your stitches out so that there are about three along each edge and one at the point where the ring and outer edge touch. At the four points shown in figure 58, attach one Victorian Gold seed bead with G as you oversew the edges.

### Assembling the star

**1.** Bend each star carefully along the middle to form a right angle (figure 59).

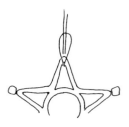

*Figure 60: Joining the star*

*Figure 59: Where to bend the star*

2. Measure a length of invisible thread twice the length with which you would normally work. Holding the two ends together, thread both ends through the needle so that a loop is formed at the end.

3. Hold the two star shapes together so that the folded edges touch. Insert the needle through the apex of each star immediately below the oversewn wire. Before pulling

the thread right through, slip the needle through the loop at the end. This should join the two halves together at the top with a slipknot (figure 60). Take a very small stitch in the oversewing to secure.

4. Thread one Victorian Gold glass seed bead on the needle and stitch to the top of the star, in such a way that it sits on top of both bent points.

5. Carefully run the thread down through the fabric of the top point (use one or two tiny

*Figure 61: The finished star*

running stitches) so that you have created a tiny seam joining the two halves (figure 61).

6. Carry the thread around the tops of the two rings, then pass it down between them into the ring space.

7. Thread the cut crystal bead and, if space allows, one Victorian Gold seed bead, securing the thread at the bottom of the ring.

8. Stitch the two halves of the star together firmly at the base. Secure the thread but do not cut it off—leave ends of about 10 cm (4 inches) hanging.

9. Take all the loose threads and bind them around the top of the stalk for about 10 mm (⅜ inch) as shown in figure 61. Tie off and cut off ends close to knot. Your star is now ready to be inserted in the top of the tree.

# *Finishing steps*

## SIDE SEAM

Use a sewing thread that matches the colour of the foundation fabric.

This seam is stitched in stages to allow completion of the embroidery and beading that overlaps and hides the seam in places. This staged joining is particularly important towards the top of the tree where adding embellishment will be difficult once the seam has been completed. Refer to figure 53.

1. Matching the side edges of the foundation shape and starting a few millimetres from the top (to allow for later insertion of the star), carefully oversew the edges together, taking note of above. Join the first two or three centimetres of the seam and secure the thread. Stitch the fill-in stars that cover the seam between this point and the top.

Continue to join the seam section by section, adding embellishments to the seam section by section.

2. Apply Ball 12 and finish in the same way as the other balls.

3. Attach the candy cane by stitching between the beads and across the wire along the length of the cane. Using KR003, make a bow on the shaft of the

*Figure 62: Position of bow on candy cane*

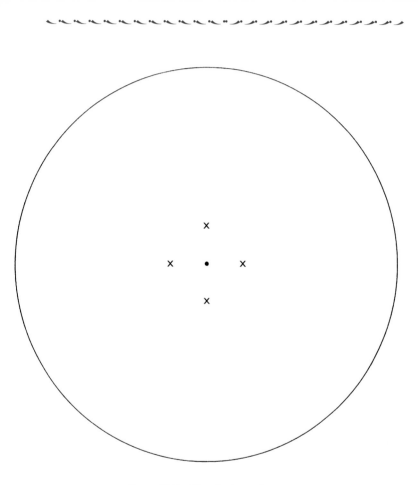

Figure 63: Template for base of tree

cane (figure 62), following the directions given for the bows on the bells on page 66.

## BASE

1. Trace the circular shape of the base (figure 63) onto template plastic or firm cardboard.

2. Cut out, keeping edges as smooth as possible.

3. Mark centre point of disk, drawing lines through the centre to about 10 mm (⅜ inch) each side to form a cross. Pierce plastic with a pin at centre and the four points at the ends of the cross.

4. Cover with green foundation fabric in the same way as for balls.

5. Using a contrasting thread, stitch a cross through the holes pierced in the plastic, on the right side of the base, to mark the centre. This provides a guide for placement of the tub centrally on the base.

## STUFFING THE TREE

1. Break the fibre-fill into small tufts and begin stuffing at the point of the tree. Push the fill in firmly.

2. Gradually add more fill, pushing it into the cone shape firmly as you go. Adding small amounts at a time will give you a smoother and more compact finish than if you add large wads at a time. Continue stuffing until the fill is nearly level with the lower edge.

3. With the right side facing out, place the base on the lower edge of the cone and begin attaching the base to the tree. Use small oversewing stitches, joining the two shapes until you have worked around about two-thirds of the base.

4. Add more fill and push this into the area now joined.

**5.** Continue stitching and adding small amounts of fill until the seam is joined and a firm shape has been achieved.

## ATTACHING THE STAR

Insert the bound stalks of the star into the space left at the apex of the tree. The presence of the filling means you will need to slide the stalk down between the filling and the inside of the tree. Trim ends if stalks are too long. Secure by taking a few small stitches at the top of the tree.

## TUB

Apply a thin layer of PVC glue to the surface of the tub. Starting at the bottom, gently wind the golden yellow ribbon floss around the tub until it is completely and evenly covered. Allow to dry.

Glue the tub to the centre of the tree base.

## CARING FOR YOUR TREE

Once you have finished your tree you will find that admirers will want to pick it up and feel it. Isn't this something most of us do when we see something we like? Sitting the tree under glass is one way to discourage handling and will, at the same time, protect it from dust and other airborne nasties! A glass dome similar to those used for carriage clocks is ideal, particularly if it comes with a base. An upturned large cylindrical glass vase is another solution. At present I use a large candle-holder made of fine glass which, turned upside down, covers the tree nicely. The tree sits on a thick cork mat covered in black flocked paper and the glass fits snugly over this. This arrangement has enabled my tree to survive being a shop counter display for three years.

Few guarantees can be made about how much fading over time is likely to occur, particularly with the fabrics used in this project. Storage out of the light from Christmas to Christmas is recommended. Wrap your tree carefully in acid-free tissue paper, taking care to protect and support the treetop star. Store in a sturdy box with a firm-fitting lid in a place away from the light.

# Stitch glossary

## Alternating chain stitch

## Backstitch

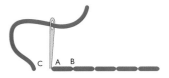

## Chain stitch

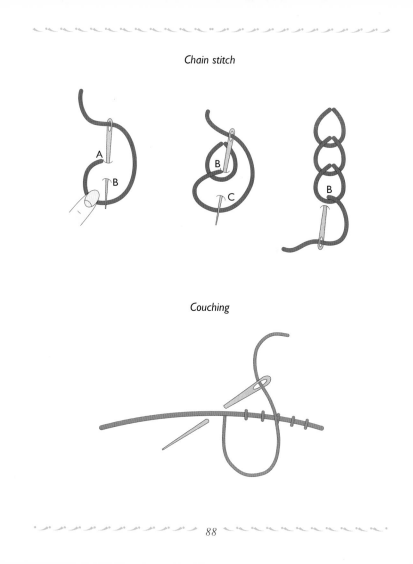

## Couching

## Double buttonhole stitch

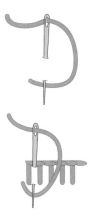

## Feather stitch

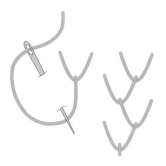

*Fly stitch*

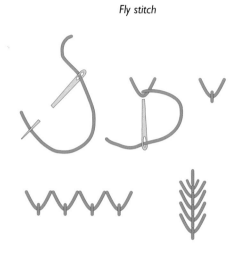

*French knot*

## Lazy Daisy

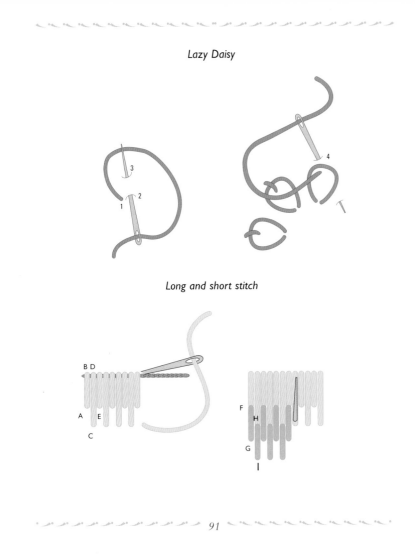

## Long and short stitch

## Satin stitch

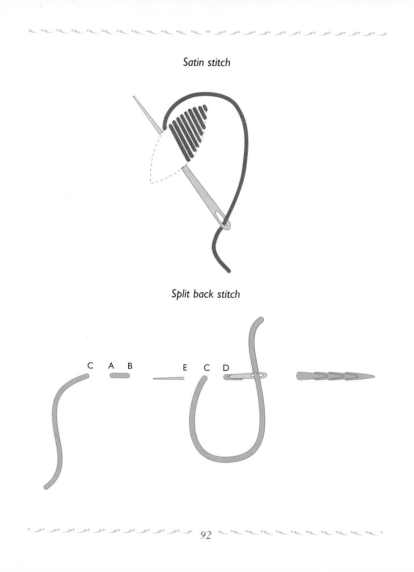

## Split back stitch

## Star stitch

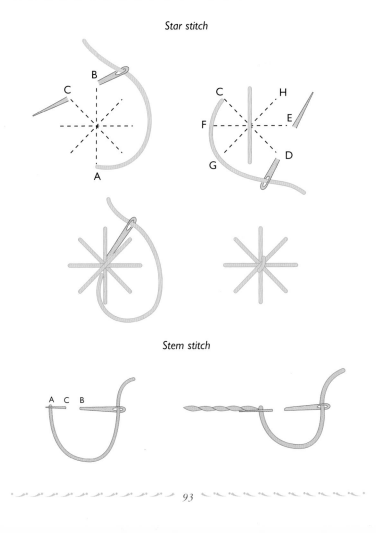

## Stem stitch

## Straight stitch

## Trellis couching

# Embroidery thread equivalents

If the Rajmahal threads used in this project are not readily available, as sometimes happens, the DMC stranded threads listed in the table are close equivalents.

| RAJMAHAL | DMC |
|---|---|
| 29 Charcoal | 310 Black |
| 96 White | White |
| 44 Tangier Sand | 3046 Rye Beige |
| 45 Baby Camel | 729 Honey Gold |
| 113 Purple Dusk | 553 Amethyst Violet |
| 126 Royal Blue | 820 Marine Blue |
| 152 Spring Leaf | 702 Fresh Green |
| 175 Earth | 938 Espresso Brown |
| 181 Gentle Magenta | 3608 Medium Pink Plum |
| 255 Vermilion | 816 Red Fruit |
| 788 Perfect Blue | 995 Caribbean Blue |

# Suppliers

Stores stocking bridal and evening wear fabrics are those most likely to stock the range of fabrics used in this project. As only small quantities are required these may also be found in your existing stash or remnant bag. A visit to your local recycled clothing or charity shop may also be productive.

Threads produced by DMC, Kreinik and Rajmahal are available in most specialist embroidery shops. Seed, Delica, bugle and pearl beads are readily available from specialist bead shops, with Mill Hill beads often being stocked by those selling embroidery supplies.

Craft and specialist bead shops stock sequins. Gütterman produce a wide range of colours in sizes 6–10 mm, which are available from craft and some embroidery outlets.

A kit containing all requirements, with the exception of fibre-fill, is available from the following suppliers (content may vary slightly depending on availability).

Samplers and Sew On
PO Box 2161
Churchlands
Western Australia 6018
Phone/fax 61 8 9287 1657
email: jensteph@iinet.net.au

Ivy and Maude
1a Station Street
Cottesloe
Western Australia 6011
Phone 61 8 9384 4225
Fax 61 8 9383 4437
www.ivyandmaude.com.au